A Day at the **Beach**

Animal Life on the Shore

Beach Fleas

and Other Tiny Sand Animals

by Ellen Lawrence

Consultant:

Dr. Daniel W. Beckman
Department of Biology
Missouri State University
Springfield, Missouri

BEARPORT
PUBLISHING

New York, New York

Credits

Cover, © Alan Gregg/Alamy, © AOFTO/Shutterstock, and © Barbara Dudzinska/Shutterstock; 2, © Alan Gregg/Alamy; 4, © Camera Lucida/Alamy; 5, © blickwinkel/Alamy; 5R, © Alan Gregg/Alamy; 6, © David Chapman/Alamy; 7, © Frank Hecker/Alamy; 8, © Steve Trewhella/FLPA; 9, © Roger Wilmshurst/FLPA; 10T, © RGB Ventures/Superstock/Alamy; 10B, © Olena Z/Shutterstock; 11, © RGB Ventures/Superstock/Alamy; 12, © RGB Ventures/Superstock/Alamy; 13, © Carlyn Iverson/Science Source/Ardea; 13R, © D P Wilson/FLPA; 14, © Debra Stika; 15, © Bob Perry/Marine Bio Photography; 16, © Pavel Krasensky/Shutterstock; 17, © guraydere/Shutterstock; 18, © iceink/Shutterstock; 19, © blickwinkel/Alamy; 20, © Fabio Pupin/FLPA; 21L, © Gary K Smith/FLPA; 21R, © Marek R Swadzba/Shutterstock; 22L, © George Ostertag/Alamy; 22R, © Albert Lleal/Minden Pictures/FLPA; 23TL, © Ava Peattie/Shutterstock; 23TC, © jiraphoto/Shutterstock; 23TR, © yod67/Shutterstock; 23BL, © Ortodox/Shutterstock; 23BC, © imageBROKER/Alamy; 23BR, © D P Wilson/FLPA.

Publisher: Kenn Goin
Senior Editor: Joyce Tavolacci
Creative Director: Spencer Brinker
Photo Researcher: Ruth Owen Books

Library of Congress Cataloging-in-Publication Data

Names: Lawrence, Ellen, 1967– author.
Title: Beach fleas and other tiny sand animals / by Ellen Lawrence.
Description: New York, New York : Bearport Publishing, [2018] | Series: At the beach
Identifiers: LCCN 2017047808 (print) | LCCN 2017054815 (ebook) | ISBN 9781684025077 (Ebook) | ISBN 9781684024490 (library)
Subjects: LCSH: Seashore animals—Juvenile literature. | Beaches—Juvenile literature.
Classification: LCC QL122.2 (ebook) | LCC QL122.2 .L3845 2018 (print) | DDC 591.769/9—dc23
LC record available at https://lccn.loc.gov/2017047808

For more information, write to Bearport Publishing Company, Inc., 45 West 21st Street, Suite 3B, New York, New York 10010. Printed in the United States of America.

10 9 8 7 6 5 4 3 2 1

Contents

Meet the Beach Fleas

A beach is often home to seals, seagulls, and crabs.

Did you know that it's also home to millions of tiny animals, including beach fleas?

These mini-creatures bury themselves in the sand under seaweed.

Lift up a piece of seaweed, and dozens of beach fleas may be hiding underneath!

Beach fleas are also known as sand hoppers or beach hoppers. How do you think they got their name?

students studying beach fleas

A beach flea is a type of tiny **crustacean**. It has an outer shell and a body that's made up of segments, or sections.

segments

beach fleas

Clean-Up Crew

A beach flea, or sand hopper, is less than I inch (2.5 cm) long.

It may be tiny, but it's an excellent jumper.

Boing! It can leap 3 feet (0.9 m) in a single jump!

During the day, a beach flea often burrows into the sand.

This keeps its body from drying out in the sun.

At night, it looks for dead seaweed and plants to eat.

beach fleas buried in sand

a beach flea eating seaweed

Beach fleas help clean up dead, smelly seaweed that covers some beaches. They may be tiny, but there are lots of them to do the work.

Why do you think being a good jumper is helpful to a beach flea?

Beach Life

In summer, male and female beach fleas meet up to **mate**.

The female lays eggs and then carries them on her back.

Weeks later, when baby beach fleas hatch, they can't yet burrow into sand.

Therefore, they spend their days hiding under damp seaweed.

By the time winter comes, however, they're able to burrow like adults.

a beach flea buried in sand

Beach fleas have lots of enemies, including birds, insects, and crabs.

beach fleas

rock pipit

9

Mole Crabs

A beach may also be home to other small crustaceans known as mole crabs.

These little creatures spend their lives buried in wet sand.

As the tide rises and falls, they move up and down the beach.

They like to be in soft sand beneath the swash.

That's the frothy water where the waves break.

mole crab

swash

eyes on stalks

shell

A mole crab is about 1.5 inches (3.8 cm) long. It has five pairs of hairy legs and two eyes on stalks.

leg

Sea Food!

A mole crab uses its hairy legs to burrow backward into soft sand.

The little creature is a fast digger—it can disappear under the sand in less than two seconds!

Once the tide washes over the beach, the animal pokes its head out.

Then it grabs food from the water with its two feathery **antennae**.

A mole crab feeds mostly on tiny floating plants and animals called **plankton**.

a mole crab burrowing into sand

Hiding under the sand keeps mole crabs safe from seabirds and other predators.

antennae

a mole crab catching food in the water

tiny plankton viewed through a microscope

How do you think mole crabs got their name?
(The answer is on page 24.)

Baby Mole Crabs

A female mole crab mates with a male crab about once a month.

After mating, she lays thousands of tiny orange eggs.

She carries the eggs on the underside of her body.

Tiny baby crabs called **larvae** hatch from the eggs and float in the sea.

the underside of a female mole crab

eggs

a greatly magnified
mole crab larva

Over time,
a mole crab larva
grows bigger and changes
shape. After about four
months, it looks like a tiny
adult and is ready to live
on a beach.

Fierce Antlions

On many beaches, there are sandy hills called sand dunes.

Hiding in the dunes is a fierce **insect**—the antlion!

A female antlion lays her eggs in the sand, among leaves, or on dry wood.

A fat larva with enormous jaws hatches from each egg.

It's hungry and ready to hunt.

adult antlion

An adult antlion has a long, thin body and two pairs of wings. There are about 2,000 different kinds of antlions.

antlion larva

jaws

17

A Deadly Trap

An antlion larva digs a pit in the soft sand.

Then it buries itself at the bottom of the pit and waits.

When an ant or other small insect walks over the trap, it falls in!

That's when the larva's big jaws poke through the sand to grab the insect.

Then the larva drags its victim beneath the sand.

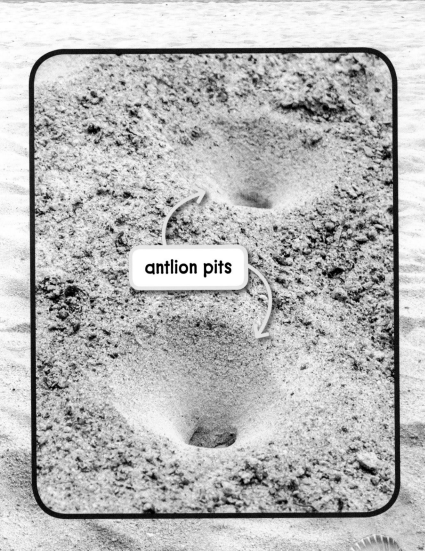

antlion pits

18

a trapped ant

Once an insect falls into an antlion's trap, it may try to climb out and escape. Then the antlion larva flicks sand at its victim. This knocks the insect back to the bottom of the pit.

antlion

Dinner in the Dunes

In its sandy trap, the antlion larva starts to feed.

It sucks the juices from its victim's body.

Finally, it flicks its prey's dead, dry body out of the trap.

Then the antlion larva buries itself again at the bottom of its pit.

Here it waits for its next meal.

a larva burrowing backward into the sand

After two or three years, an antlion larva makes itself a sandy case, or cocoon. Inside its cocoon, it changes into an adult with wings.

an antlion cocoon

adult antlion

21

Science Lab

Be a Beach Creature Scientist!

Scientists have studied tiny beach animals for many years. Now it's your turn to investigate! Read the following questions and write your answers in a notebook.

I. Which of the animals in this book do you think made these trails on a beach? How?

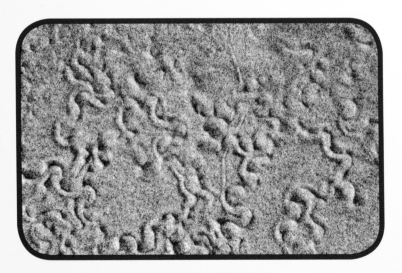

2. This photo of an antlion larva and an ant was taken using a powerful microscope. What do you think is happening in the picture?

3. Write one paragraph about the life of a beach flea. Try to use the following words:

crustacean   seaweed

shell   eggs   jump

(The answers are on page 24.)

Science Words

antennae (an-TEN-ee) two long, thin body parts on an animal's head used for feeling, smelling, or finding food

crustacean (kruhs-TAY-shuhn) an animal with a shell and no backbone that often lives in water

insect (IN-sekt) a small animal with six legs, a body with three parts, antennae, and a hard covering called an exoskeleton

larvae (LAR-vee) the young of some animals, including insects and crustaceans

mate (MAYT) to come together to produce young

plankton (PLANGK-tuhn) tiny animals and plants that float in oceans, lakes, and ponds

Index

Read More

Burnie, David. *Seashore: Explore Nature with Fun Facts and Activities.* New York: DK (2017).

Owen Ruth. *Welcome to the Seashore (Nature's Neighborhoods: All About Ecosystems).* New York: Ruby Tuesday (2016).

Parker, Steve. *Seashore (DK Eyewitness Books).* New York: DK (2004).

Learn More Online

To learn more about beach fleas and other tiny sand animals, visit **www.bearportpublishing.com/ADayAtTheBeach**

About the Author

Ellen Lawrence lives in the United Kingdom. Her favorite books to write are those about nature and animals. In fact, the first book Ellen bought for herself when she was six years old was the story of a gorilla named Patty Cake that was born in New York's Central Park Zoo.

Answers

Page 13: Mole crabs got their name because they burrow underground like the moles that live beneath gardens and fields. Mole crabs aren't actually crabs, but they belong to the same animal group as crabs.

Page 22:

1. The trails on the beach were made by mole crabs moving around under the sand.

2. The antlion larva is gripping an ant in its jaws. The larva is feeding on the ant by sucking juices from its body.